B is for Buckaroo

A Cowboy Alphabet

Written by Louise Doak Whitney & Gleaves Whitney
Illustrated by Susan Guy

Sleeping Bear Press™
2395 South Huron Parkway, Suite 200
Ann Arbor, MI 48104
www.sleepingbearpress.com

Printed and bound in the United States.

15 14 13 (case)
16 15 14 13 (pbk)

Library of Congress Cataloging-in-Publication Data
Whitney, Gleaves.
B is for buckaroo : a cowboy alphabet / by Gleaves Whitney and Louise Doak
Whitney ; illustrated by Susan Guy.
p. cm.
Summary: The letters of the alphabet are represented by words, set in short
rhymes with additional information, relating to cowboys and ranch life.

pbk ISBN-13: 978-1-58536-336-0   case ISBN-13: 978-1-58536-139-7

1. Cowboys-West (U.S.)—Juvenile literature. 2. Ranch life-West (U.S.)—Juvenile
literature. 3. West (U.S.)—Social life and customs-Juvenile literature. 4. English
language-Alphabet-Juvenile literature. [1. Cowboys-West (U.S.) 2. Ranch life-
West (U.S.) 3. West (U.S.)—Social life and customs. 4. Alphabet.] I. Whitney,
Louise Doak. II. Guy, Susan, 1948- ill. III. Title.
F596 .W567 2003
978—dc22   2003013207

For three boys who love the spirit of the West—
Ian, Alasdair, and Andrew

GLEAVES & LOUISE

To my wonderful husband and family, thank you for
all your love and support. I couldn't do it without you.
Thank you also to Sleeping Bear Press.
It's great working with you.

SUE

Note to the reader: Because the ranching tradition has roots in medieval Spain,
many of the words we associate with cowboy ways come from Spanish.
We have highlighted these words and hope you enjoy learning about them.

Andalusia is in southern Spain, where ranching and cowboy culture began hundreds of years before Columbus sailed to the Americas. Later in the fifteenth century when the Spanish came to the New World, they brought with them cattle—ancestors of the Texas longhorns—and their knowledge of ranching. The Spaniards introduced cowboy ways in Mexico. Later when the Anglo-American pioneers went west, Mexican cowboys taught the early settlers how to take care of cattle from horseback. The Spanish influence can be seen in many cowboy words and customs to this day. Wrangler comes from a Spanish word—*caballerango*—that means a man on a horse.

The American cowboy was first seen in Texas in the 1850s. American settlers learned from their Mexican neighbors how to take care of the longhorn cattle that roamed wild and free.

When the Civil War ended slavery in the United States, many newly freed African-Americans began their life of freedom working as cowboys.

Andalusia begins with an A—
Spanish land that's far away.
It's where our story begins
of the colorful cowboy way.

The word buckaroo comes from the Spanish name for cowboy, which is *vaquero*. If you say "vaquero" and "buckaroo," you will hear that they sound similar.

A cowboy is someone who tends cattle, usually from horseback. Cowboys do many jobs including watching over cattle as they graze on the prairie, rounding them up to bring them into the corral, taking care of them when they are sick, branding them to identify ownership, and working with the horses that are the cowboy's partners.

B is also for bronc or *bronco*, Spanish for a wild, unbroken horse—a mustang that is not ready for riding. Broncos were descended from the Arabian horses that Spanish explorers brought with them to the New World. Found running wild on the plains, these horses had to be "broken" by cowboys who would train them to be good working partners. A highly skilled cowboy that can break a horse is called a broncobuster.

B is for the Buckaroo,
  who's a cowboy through and through.
These broncobusters you'll often see
  riding on horseback, yelling "Whoopee!"

Chuck wagon starts with the letter C.
It's the place where cowboys like to be,
to enjoy tasty vittles and a cup of coffee,
and tell tall tales out on the prairie.

CHARLES GOODNIGHT

The chuck wagon was named after its founder, Charles (Chuck) Goodnight, a Texas cattle rancher. Goodnight knew that cowboys on long trail rides like to eat tasty vittles (food). The chuck wagon was where the cook, often-called Cookie, prepared meals. Dinners included stews, baked beans, and biscuits. The cowboys treated Cookie with great respect, for they knew that if Cookie got upset, he might "accidentally" burn the beans or biscuits!

Jerky is a popular trail snack for cowboys. It is thin strips of meat that are dried and salted. Because jerky keeps almost forever and is light to carry, cowboys like to keep it in their packs to nibble on.

D is for the Dally
    the drovers like to make,
when they need a little dogie
    to put on the brake!

When cowboys are roping cattle, they often need to "dally," or wrap their rope around the saddle horn. The dally helps the cowboy control a cow on the other end of the rope. The Spanish *vaqueros*, who used the term *dale vuelta* to describe wrapping their rope around the saddle horn, invented dallying.

Drover is another name for cowboy, because a cowboy *drove* cattle on the trail drive. Dogie, not to be confused with a little dog or doggie, is another word for calf.

Cowboy work is dangerous. One of the biggest dangers a cowboy could face is a stampede, the wild, chaotic running of cattle on a trail drive. It is hard to predict what might cause a stampede, but lightning, tumbleweeds, a coyote call, or rattlesnake might spook the cattle and cause them to run wild. It was what all cowboys feared the most because it was dangerous and difficult to get the cattle under control. Cowboys would race on their horses to head the cattle off and get them to turn direction. With care the herd could then be circled around and slowed down.

Dd

Ee

E is for the Endless plains
stretching as far as the eye can see.
For cowboys and cattle it was home,
the land that gave them room to roam.

Endless plains refer to the Great Plains, where most cowboys worked in the old days and continue to work today. These great grasslands were crisscrossed by most of the cattle drives from the 1860s to the 1880s.

The Great Plains extend all the way from Canada south to Texas and include the Canadian provinces of Alberta, Saskatchewan, and British Columbia, plus the Northwest Territories, and the states of Montana, North and South Dakota, Wyoming, Nebraska, Colorado, Kansas, New Mexico, Oklahoma, and Texas.

Grama, buffalo, crested wheat, and little bluestem are some of the tasty and nutritious grasses that grazing animals love to eat.

E is also for the equipment or "tack" that cowboys use with their horses. This includes the saddle, which is the cowboy's most valued possession. Stirrups are used to anchor the rider's feet while riding. The bit and bridle help the cowboy control the horse. Ropes are used to lasso cattle. A quirt, which is a riding whip used to train a horse or direct it, comes from the Spanish word *cuarta*. Spurs, from the Spanish word *espuela*, are used to urge the horse to run faster.

In early pioneer days, land was divided by planting thorny shrubs. Wood was scarce on the plains so wooden fences were rare. Inspired by a fence exhibit at the DeKalb, Illinois county fair, a man named Joseph Glidden developed barbed wire fencing in 1874, and the Frying Pan Ranch in Texas was the first to use it. There are many different types of barbed wire.

Farmers who wanted to protect their crops saw fencing in cattle as a good thing. But it meant the end of the open range that was so much a part of cowboy lore.

F is for the Frying Pan—
A ranch with a funny name.
    It's where the barbed wire fence began
and Joseph Glidden earned his fame.

Ff

G is for all the Gear
that cowboys like to wear—
Boots, hats, jeans, and chaps
as they work and ride the frontier.

Cowboy gear includes everything a cowboy needs to do his job. Some of the most important gear is the clothing they wear. In addition to a hat, cowboys also wear bandanas, belts, jeans, chaps, dusters, and boots.

What a cowboy wears on his feet is mighty important! Boots made of leather keep feet dry when the trail is wet and muddy, and warm when it is cold and snowy. Cowboy boots are tall to protect legs from snakes and stickers. The heels are high to keep the foot secure in the stirrup. The toes are pointed so that if a cowboy falls from the horse, the boot won't catch in the stirrup.

Chaps, also called leggings, are made of leather or canvas to protect a cowboy's legs while working in thorny bushes. Chaps were adapted from the *chaparajas* worn by the *vaqueros*. Short chaps are called chinks, from the Spanish *chincadera*.

Usually made from buckskin, gauntlets are the big gloves worn to help protect hands from blisters, cold, and rope burns.

H h

In Spanish *vaquero* days, the cowboy hat was called a *sombrero*. Later, as a joke, John B. Stetson created a big umbrella-like hat in the 1860s that looked funny but kept the sun, rain, and snow off the cowboy's head. He called it the "Boss of the Plains." Cowboys really liked his hat, and soon orders came in from ranchers, trail bosses, cowpokes, and Texas Rangers.

Hats are one of the most distinctive cowboy emblems and can be made of felt, leather, or straw. A cowboy hat is usually the first thing on in the morning and the last thing off at night.

Hats are our letter H–
Keeping off the sun, rain, and snow.
With a tall crown and wide brim,
they sure do make a show.

The blacksmith uses an anvil and white-hot iron to forge horseshoes. Horseshoes were once the most important thing the smith made. Horses need shoes or their hooves will crack and cause pain. Then the horse can't be ridden. A horse's hooves grow, so every four to six weeks, a horse needs to be fitted for new shoes. A farrier is a blacksmith who specializes in horseshoes. "Farrier" comes from the Latin word for iron.

A branding iron puts a mark—usually a letter, number, or symbol—on the hide of a cow or horse. Done properly, branding does not hurt the animal. Cowboys brand cattle to show who owns them in case they roam. Each ranch has its own brand and they are fun to learn how to read. The "lazy I" brand, for example, lies on its side. The "walking I" has two little legs. You could think of a brand as the return address for a cow!

Iron starts with the letter I,
white hot from the fire.
An iron horseshoe and iron brand
the blacksmith forges by hand.

Cowboys make quite an impression when they walk into a room with spurs on, especially if they are wearing jinglebobs! These little bells dangle from the back of the spur and are just a fun decoration.

J is also for jollification—a word used by cowboys and cowgirls when they have fun. A jollification on a trail drive might be listening to harmonica or fiddle music and dancing.

J j

Jinglebob begins with the letter J—
It's the little bell on a spur,
jingling, jangling all day,
especially when cowboys dance and play.

King Ranch begins with the letter K.
    It's where American ranching began.
To learn about the cowboy way,
    visit this spread if you can.

The word ranch comes from the Spanish *ranchero* and means a large farm where cattle, horses, and sheep are raised. The King Ranch near Kingsville, Texas, is the birthplace of American ranching (but not the birthplace of Spanish or Mexican ranching). Established in 1853, it remains one of the largest working ranches in the United States. It is still owned by the King family.

Kineños is the Spanish word for the people who came from a village in Mexico to help Richard King work the land. They adopted King's name since they worked for his family.

Now let's lasso some L words....

L is for Lariat or Lasso,
a loop of rope coiled just so.
Swing it wide or swing it low.
Hook those longhorns and yell "Whoa!"

Whenever you see a working cowboy on a horse, you'll also see a rope that is coiled and hanging from the saddle horn. The Spanish *vaqueros* called the rope *la reata*, which became our word "lariat." A lasso or lariat is a long leather or hemp rope that is used to rope a cow. It takes a lot of practice to learn how to rope and ride at the same time. Cowboys will rope animals in order to brand them, "doctor" them, or help them if they get stuck in the mud!

L is also for longhorns, the mean, wild cattle of Texas. Descended from the old mission cattle brought to Mexico from Spain, longhorns can weigh as much as a car and can have horns as wide as six feet across!

Besides longhorns, you will see other famous breeds of cattle as you drive past ranches. You can recognize them by their color. Santa Gertrudis cattle are dark red-brown. Brahman are typically light gray. Herefords are red and white. Charolais are all white. Can you guess the color of a Black Angus cow?

Ll

Mesteño is Spanish for "mustang," a wild horse that runs free. You can still find herds of them in Nevada, Wyoming, and Montana. Their ancestors were brought to the New World by the Spaniard explorers.

Ask any cowboy or cowgirl and they will tell you that a tamed, well-trained horse is not a pet, it's a partner. Cowboys favor good saddle horses, which include the American quarter horse, Appaloosa, Palomino, Arabian, and Morgan breeds.

When working cattle in a corral, a cowboy will use a cutting horse. Often a quarter horse, the cutter will gently bite the cattle on the hide, usually on the flank. This is the way the cowboy and horse work together as a team to direct traffic in the corral. He rides his horse to separate individual cows from the herd in order "to doctor" and brand them. Many rodeos feature cutting horse competitions.

M is also for mule, which is a cross between a horse and a donkey. Strong and sturdy and hard workers, even under harsh conditions, mules were often the animals that pulled the chuck wagon.

Mesteño starts with the letter M—
It's a mustang, a horse wild and free.
Hard work and time will tame it
so a faithful partner it can be.

N n

Under the moonlit, starry night,
rode the Night herd, our letter N.
Cowboys keeping watch over the cattle
would sometimes nod off in the saddle!

The Night herd is a group of cowboys who ride around the sleeping cattle to keep them quiet. Cowboys on the night shift ride two hours and use the night horse, an animal with great night vision and known to be surefooted. The horse is so well trained that if the cowboy falls asleep, the horse will continue on the rounds. Sometimes as they ride around the herd, the cowboys will sing softly or whistle so the cattle know there is no danger.

Annie Oakley was a famous cowgirl who toured North America and Europe in Buffalo Bill's *Wild West Show*. Sitting Bull nicknamed her "Little Sure Shot." She was best known for her ability to shoot a gun with dead-on accuracy. When not performing, her hobby was needlework.

There have been many women who worked as cowgirls, helping with ranching chores such as caring for the horses and branding. Women also rode the range, herded cattle, and helped to care for sick and injured livestock. In today's rodeos, women compete in barrel racing, which is a high-speed ride around several barrels in an arena. The woman who completes the race in the shortest time without overturning a barrel is the winner.

At the Cowgirl Hall of Fame in Fort Worth, Texas, you can learn about the many women who made special contributions to the life of the West.

MISS ANNIE OAKLEY
THE PEERLESS LADY WING-SHOT

Annie Oakley is the letter O,
the star of Buffalo Bill's *Wild West Show*.
"Little Sure Shot" was her nickname—
Her sharp shooting brought her fame.

Pp

One of the most colorful characters in cowboy lore is the mythical Pecos Bill. According to his legend, on a trip west, he fell out of a wagon and was raised by coyotes. Once, while in Oklahoma, Pecos Bill rode a cyclone without a saddle. The cyclone couldn't throw him, so it rained so long and hard that floodwaters created the Grand Canyon! Cowboys like to say that Pecos Bill was the inventor of roping and branding, and started the tradition of singing cowboy songs to soothe restless cattle on the trail.

His creator is unknown, however, it might be said that the tale of Pecos Bill and other Western legends sprang from the stories and songs shared around countless campfires.

Pecos Bill starts with the letter P.
The original cowboy legend was he.
He rode a cyclone without a saddle
and sang songs to quiet the cattlc.

One of the most famous American quarter horses, Old Sorrel was foaled at the King Ranch in Texas in 1915. The quarter horse is truly an original American breed. It was so named because it ran fast in the quarter-mile race. This horse is a favorite of cowboys and cowgirls because of its many qualities such as "cow sense," which means it knows what cattle are likely to do. In addition, it is sturdy and can make the quick moves needed to be a good cutting horse, while having a gentle disposition, which makes it a good family horse.

Old Sorrel sired many horses but one in particular, Wimpy, went on to become the first horse registered with the American Quarter Horse Association in 1941.

Q q

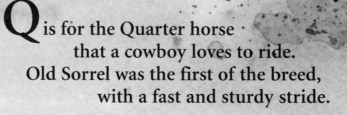

Q is for the Quarter horse
that a cowboy loves to ride.
Old Sorrel was the first of the breed,
with a fast and sturdy stride.

Rr

Riding the bulls or roping calves,
let's round up an **R** for Rodeo.
Cowboy clowns and bucking broncos
put on a ripsnortin' show!

In the early days, cattle were free to roam and graze on the grasslands. But in the spring, cowboys would gather or "round up" the herd for doctoring and branding. The word rodeo comes from the Spanish *rodear*, which means to surround or encompass.

Rodeos began in 1888 when cowboys gathered after the day's work to show off their roping and riding skills. Today many towns come alive for the rodeo. In Canada, the Calgary Stampede, held in Calgary, Alberta, is billed as the "largest outdoor rodeo" and is an annual 10-day event. Every official rodeo includes five standard events: bull riding, saddle bronc riding, calf roping, bulldogging, and bareback riding. Barrel racing is the only women's event and is sometimes included in the rodeo. One of the best parts of the rodeo is watching the rodeo clowns, skilled riders who help protect cowboys if they fall off a bull or bronco.

Bill Pickett, an African-American cowboy born in Texas about 1870, invented the wild rodeo sport of bulldogging or steer wrestling.

Ss

S stands for Saddle
    with a horn, cinch, and cantle.
It's a throne on a horse
    for a cowboy, of course!

The saddle is the most important piece of gear or tack a cowboy or cowgirl owns. It includes the harness, bridle, and reins, all made of leather. The tree of the saddle is the wooden frame it is built on. The front of the tree is called a fork. The horn is attached to the fork and both are used to help the cowboy with roping and dallying. The back of the tree is the cantle, the curved backrest of the saddle. Underneath the saddle is the blanket that protects the horse's back. The cinch, also called a girth, is the strap on the saddle that runs underneath the horse's belly. *Tapaderos* refers to the leather coverings that fit over a stirrup and protect the rider's foot from thorny brush and cactus. The pannier is the set of bags that is strapped to the saddle and used to pack a few possessions.

The saddle has to be comfortable during the day and is often used as a pillow at night!

There were many trails the cowboys followed to move cattle from the open ranges to railroad lines in Kansas and Nebraska. The cowboys needed to take the cattle from their grazing lands to the railroad so they could be shipped to beef markets in the eastern United States.

The days of the great trail drives were from the 1860s to the 1880s. Many trails started in Texas in places such as Fort Concho, San Antonio, Austin, and Houston. Some trails were nearly 1,000 miles long and took two to three months to complete. A trail boss who managed the cook, drivers, and wranglers as they moved cattle along the trail led the trail drive. The Chisholm, Shawnee, Western, and Goodnight-Loving trails are just a few of the most famous.

Remuda is Spanish for a group of horses on a trail drive or ranch.

T is for the many Trails,
    used to herd cattle to the rails.
        With names like Goodnight and Santa Fe,
        they remain a legend to this day.

The Union Pacific Railroad was begun in 1862 to extend the existing railroad from Omaha, Nebraska, westward. Trains coming west were what started cowboys on their long trail drives from Texas. The cowboys would herd cattle to the trains and the trains would take the cattle to cities back East to feed people. Today the Union Pacific is one of the largest transportation companies in the United States with over 38,000 miles of train track!

Union Pacific is the train
that starts with the letter U.
Listen for the lonely whistle
as it crosses the plains—choo-choo!

U u

Vaquero starts with the letter V–
A Spanish cowboy was he.
Knowing how to rope and ride,
he was the first of the cowboy pride.

V v

The first cowboys in America were from Spain and called themselves *vaqueros*. (*Vaquero* comes from *vaca*, which means "cow" in Spanish.) They were the first cowboys, tending cattle from horseback. Cattle ranching and cowboying in America has roots in Spain and began when Columbus came to the New World (*Hispaniola*) for the second time in 1494. With him on that trip were horses and cattle that flourished in the New World.

A conquistador named Cortés took some of the cattle from *Hispaniola* to Mexico. As the Spanish moved north from Mexico into what is now the United States, they took cattle with them and established missions which included the first ranches, or *rancheros*. It was these mission ranches that helped feed the *padres* (priests) and Native Americans. The *vaqueros* on mission ranches taught Native Americans and early pioneers how to manage the cattle, along with such skills as riding, roping, and rounding up.

You can visit one of the early mission ranches near San Antonio, Texas, and learn more about Spanish ranching in the southwestern United States.

Will Rogers is known as the "cowboy philosopher." He was born in 1879 in Cherokee Indian territory (now Oklahoma) and worked as a cowboy for many years before becoming a writer, actor, and humorist. Will Rogers was an expert at doing fancy tricks with his lasso (while chewing gum!) and was once part of Texas Jack's *Wild West Show*. His most famous saying was "I never met a man I didn't like." The name of his horse was Soapsuds. He is often called the "Poet Lariat" of the United States and there is a statue of him in our nation's Capitol.

W is also for Westerns—the movies and books about cowboy life in the Wild West. John Wayne was probably the most popular and well-known Hollywood cowboy. Roy Rogers, the "King of the Cowboys," was a famous cowboy actor and singer. His horse "Trigger" was almost as famous as he!

W is for Will Rogers,
the king of cowboy philosophers.
He did fancy tricks with his lassos
to thrill kids at the *Wild West Show*!

JOHN WAYNE in THE SEARCHERS

The XIT Ranch is in the Texas Panhandle region, and its size at one time was nearly three million acres. In the 1880s the XIT Ranch was the largest ranch within a single fence in the United States.

There are many great ranches to visit such as George Ranch Historical Park in Richmond, Texas, where real cowboys will show you all about the life and work of the American cowboy. Another great ranch is the Grant-Kohrs Ranch in Montana, the only place in the National Park System that is dedicated to preserving the history of the frontier cattle era. You can also visit the ranches of these former American presidents: Lyndon B. Johnson's ranch in Texas and Ronald Reagan's Rancho del Cielo in California.

In western Canada, especially the provinces of Saskatchewan, British Columbia, and Alberta, generations of families have followed the ranching tradition.

X is for the ranch called the XIT,
  bigger than any other you'll see.
It's also a famous brand
  known for miles across the land.

Xx

Yodeling starts with the letter Y—
Cowboys crooning way up high.
Tunes that'll get your toes a tappin'
and keep both your hands a clappin'.

Y y

Yodeling is a style of singing that is found in traditional country western music. Jimmie Rodgers was known as the *Singing Brakeman*; he was an early country musician and developed a style of singing known as the "Blue Yodel." This was a combination of African-American blues music and country yodeling.

Music has always been a big part of the cowboy life. Sometimes at night around the campfire you could hear a tune being played on a harmonica. The harmonica is small and easy to pack and so was a favorite on the trail drive.

Did you know that a singing cowboy made some of your favorite Christmas songs popular? Gene Autry popularized "Rudolph the Red-Nosed Reindeer" and "Here Comes Santa Claus." And one of the most famous cowboy songs ever written, "Home on the Range," is the state song of Kansas.

At last we come to Zane Grey,
whose first name starts with a Z.
He wrote stories about cowboys
to be enjoyed by you and me.

Zane Grey was a famous author and many of his stories about cowboys and the Wild West became the basis of Western movies. He was ahead of his time in his respectful treatment of Native Americans. Many people believe his book, *Riders of the Purple Sage*, to be the best Western ever written. His words painted a picture of the American West that we treasure today.

Owen Wister, another famous author, wrote one of the first Westerns, *The Virginian*.

Cowboys also like to tell their stories in poetry. In the early days, cowboys would tell tall tales ("windies"), sing songs, and recite poetry around the campfire. Today, you can hear cowboy poets at the annual Cowboy Poetry gathering every January at the Western Folklife Center in Elko, Nevada, and every May at the George Ranch near Houston, Texas.

The cowboy way of life is not only told in literature but also in art. Frederic Remington and Charles Russell were two of the many artists whose paintings and sculptures of cowboys and Native Americans helped tell the story of the West.

Round Up A New Word!

Spanish Words and Their Meanings

Bronco: a wild, unbroken horse

Caballerango: wrangler, a man on a horse

Chaparajas: chaps, leather or canvas leggings worn to protect a cowboy's legs

Chincadera: chinks or short chaps

Cuarta: a quirt, a riding whip that is used to train or direct a horse

Dale vuelta: dallying, or wrapping a rope around the saddle horn to control an animal

Espuelas: spurs, used to urge the horse to run faster

La reata: a lariat or lasso, a long leather or hemp rope that is used to rope a cow

Mesteño: a mustang, a wild horse that runs free

Ranchero: a ranch, a large farm where cattle, horses, and sheep are raised

Remuda: a group of horses on a trail drive or ranch

Rodear: to surround or encompass (the word rodeo came from this)

Sombrero: a cowboy hat

Tapaderos: the leather coverings that fit over a stirrup and protect the rider's foot from thorny brush and cactus

Vaca: a cow

Vaqueros: Spanish cowboys

Acknowledgments

Just as no one makes the trail ride alone, but travels with the assistance of others, we could not have written this book without the generosity of many people who shared their expertise and enthusiasm for the cowboy way. Our gratitude goes to:

Our Texas ranching family, Aunt Caroline and Uncle Mickey Cusack, of Chisholm Trail Ranch, as well as Uncle Tommy and Aunt Mary Jane Cloud, of Cloud Canyon Ranch.

"Jim and the Cowboys" at the George Ranch Historical Park, Richmond, Texas: Jim Hodges, lead cowboy and historical interpreter; Nicholas Castelberg, chuck wagon cook; Nathan Trilicek, top hand; and cowboys Brett Haney, Kevin Powell, Cody Arnold, Brandon Parr, and John Turner; also Orin Covell, administrative officer; Bryan McAuley, director of programs; and Joan Fraser and Leigh Hurder, visitor services.

King Ranch, Kingsville, Texas

Grant-Kohrs Ranch, Deer Lodge, Montana

Flying W Ranch, Colorado Springs, Colorado

Cowboy Hall of Fame, Oklahoma City, Oklahoma

National Cowgirl Museum and Hall of Fame, Fort Worth, Texas

LBJ Ranch State Park and Historic Site, Stonewall, Texas

Lyndon B. Johnson National Historical Park, Johnson City, Texas

Rancho del Cielo and Young America's Foundation, Santa Barbara, California

Eli Paulsen at the ProRodeo Hall of Fame and Museum of the American Cowboy, Colorado Springs, Colorado

The Witte Museum, San Antonio, Texas

The Chisholm Trail Heritage Center, Duncan, Oklahoma

San Antonio Missions National Historic Park, San Antonio, Texas

La Purisima Mission State Historic Park, Lompoc, California

We thank y'all for making this book so much fun to work on.

—*Louise and Gleaves Whitney*

Louise & Gleaves Whitney

Historian Gleaves Whitney grew up in Texas where his love of the West and admiration for the cowboy way of life took root. At the age of four, he met Roy Rogers, Dale Evans, and Trigger. A graduate of Colorado State University and the University of Michigan, he is the Director of the Hauenstein Center for Presidential Studies and is currently editing a book of the great wartime speeches of American Presidents.

Louise Doak Whitney was born and raised in Colorado along the Front Range. When she was four years old, her parents took her to see Sheriff Scotty, a Colorado cowboy entertainer. A graduate of the University of Colorado and Colorado State University, her first children's book, *C is for Centennial: A Colorado Alphabet*, was also published by Sleeping Bear Press.

The husband-wife writing duo lives in East Lansing, Michigan, and, along with their three sons, enjoys traveling throughout the American West, visiting ranches every chance they get.

Susan Guy

Award-winning artist Susan Guy is known for her colorful paintings of equine and western themes. Her work is displayed in numerous galleries and exhibitions across the country, such as the prestigious Arts for the Parks competition in Jackson, Wyoming, and the American Academy of Equine Art in Lexington, Kentucky. One of her paintings is also included in the permanent collection of the Phippen Museum in Prescott, Arizona. She is a signature member of the American Academy of Women Artists.

Susan and her husband, Wesley, have three children and eight grandchildren. They share their Buffalo, Wyoming, home with their two dogs.